Late Intermediate

SOUTH DAKOTA SCENERY

Wynn-Anne Rossi

Sacred Black Hills

Buffalo Bebop

Jewel Cave

Badlands Thunderstorm

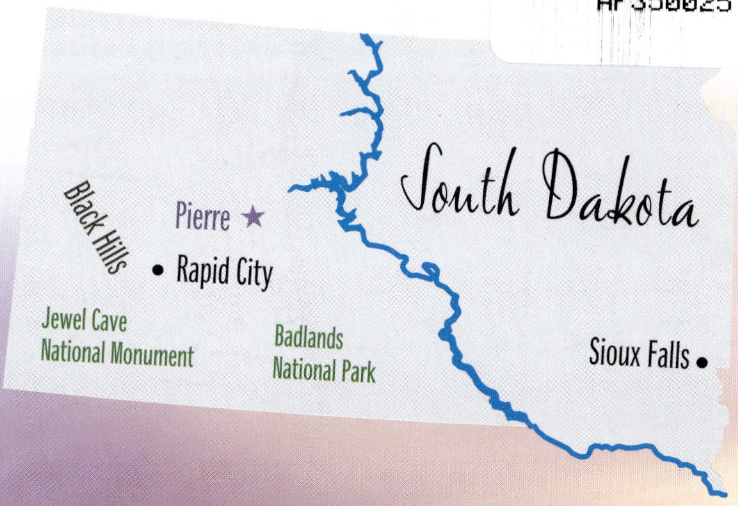

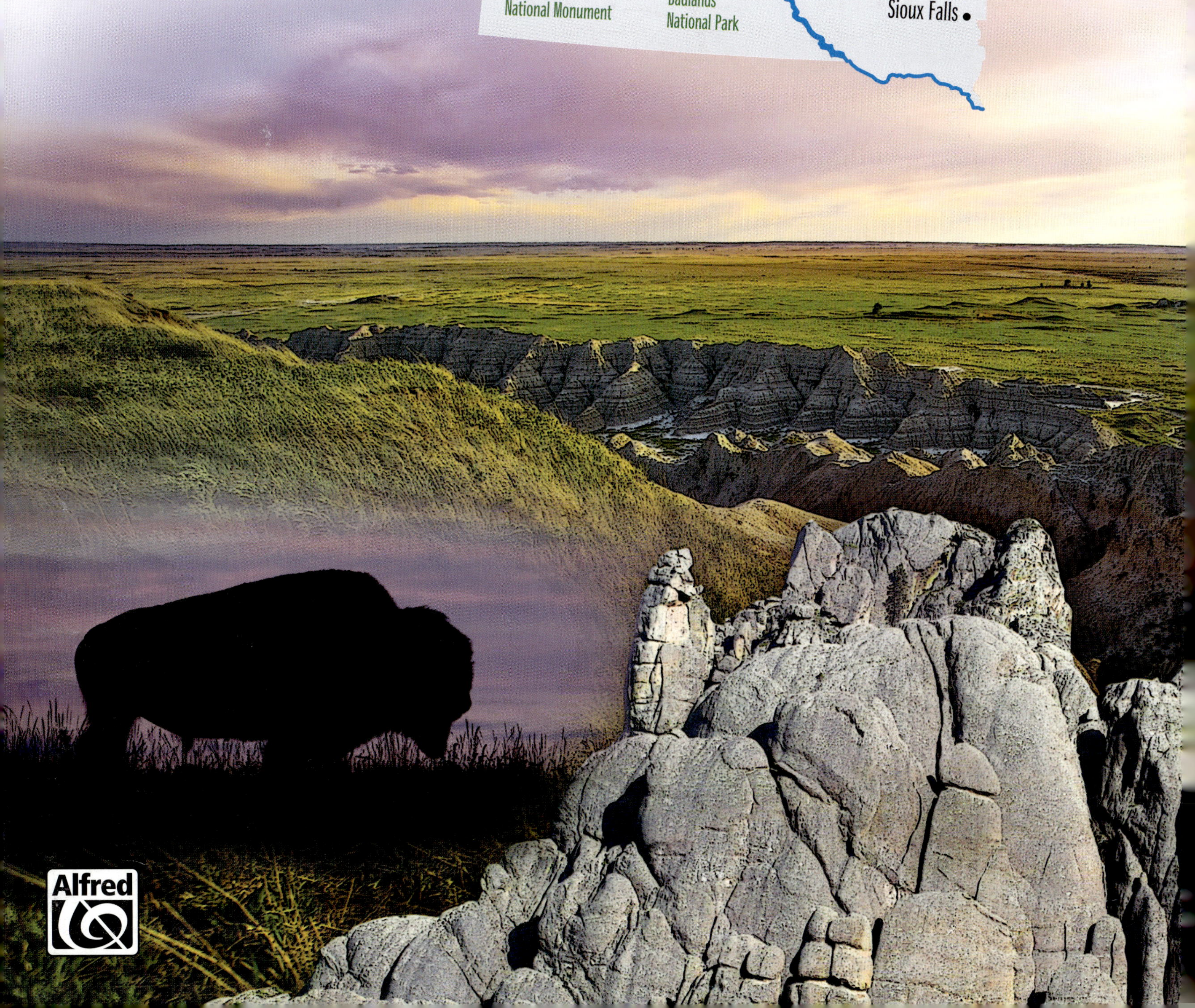

Alfred

Sacred Black Hills

For thousands of years, the Native Americans called the Black Hills (Paha Sapa) their sacred land. The march of time proved the unique value of this area, from the discovery of gold to its diverse wildlife and other natural resources. Today, the beautiful Black Hills continue to inspire great reverence and inspiration.

mf

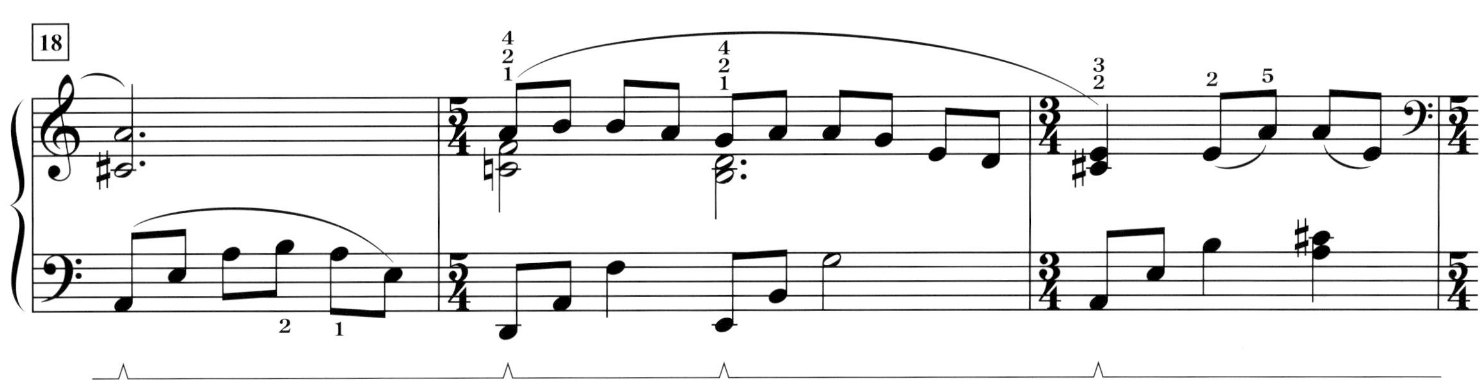

f

mp

mf

f
8va- -

mp
8va
p
pp
8va-

Buffalo Bebop

Sixty million buffalo once roamed the Great Plains. By 1889, when South Dakota became a state, the "American bison" was nearly extinct. Thankfully, they once again roam this territory in the thousands. They are still wild animals and can outrun a horse!

Wynn-Anne Rossi

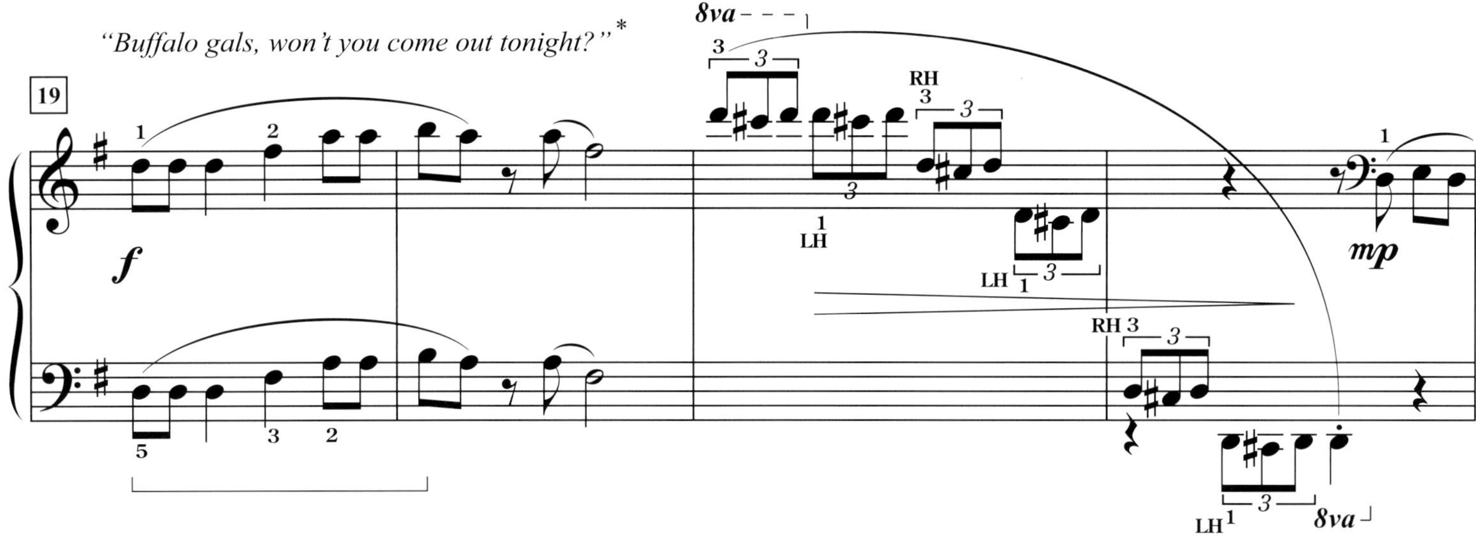

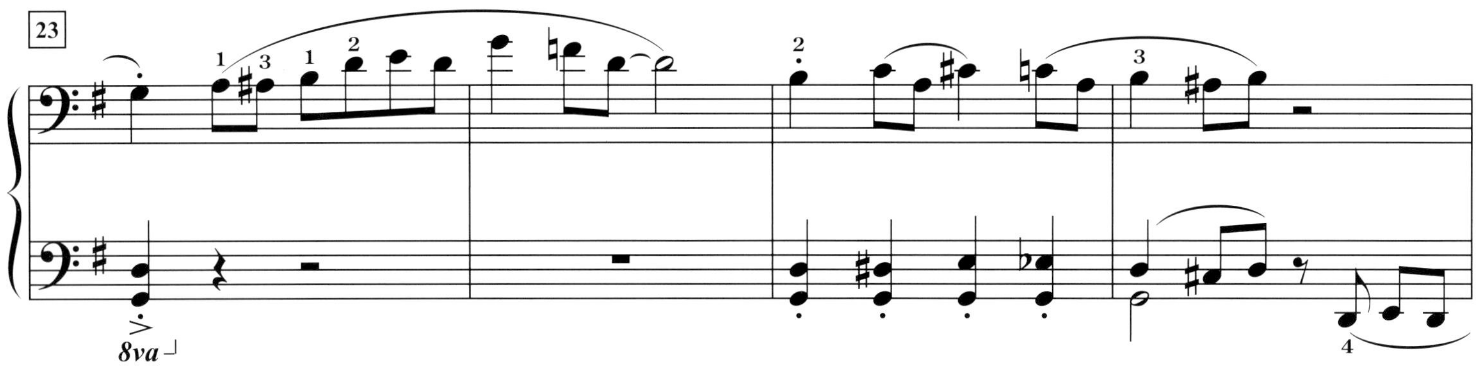

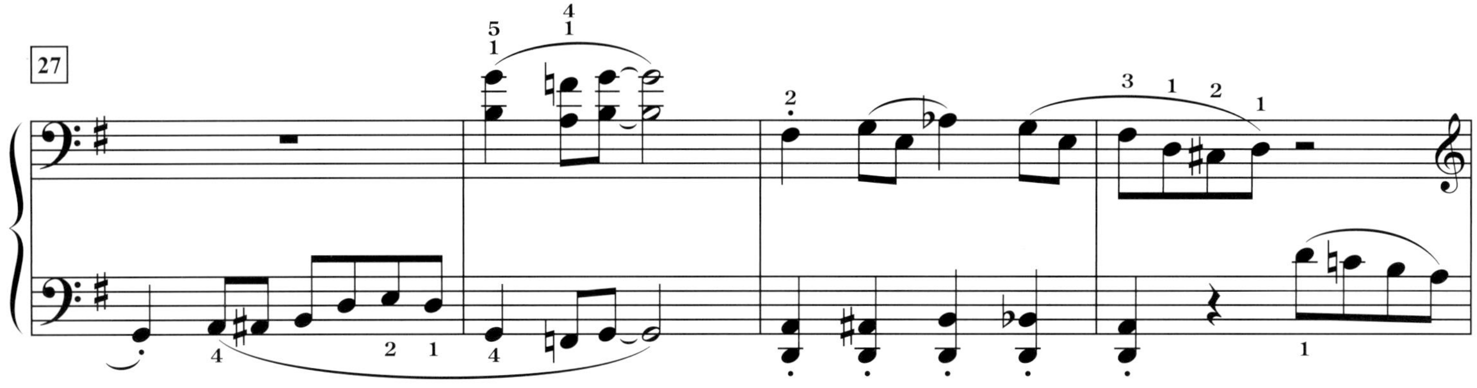

* Melody and lyrics from the traditional American song "Buffalo Gals"

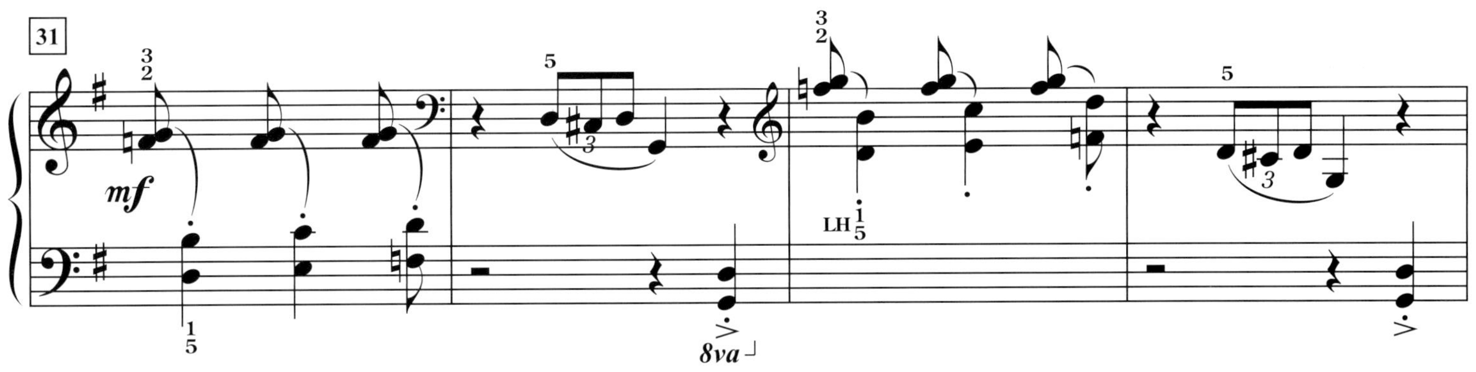

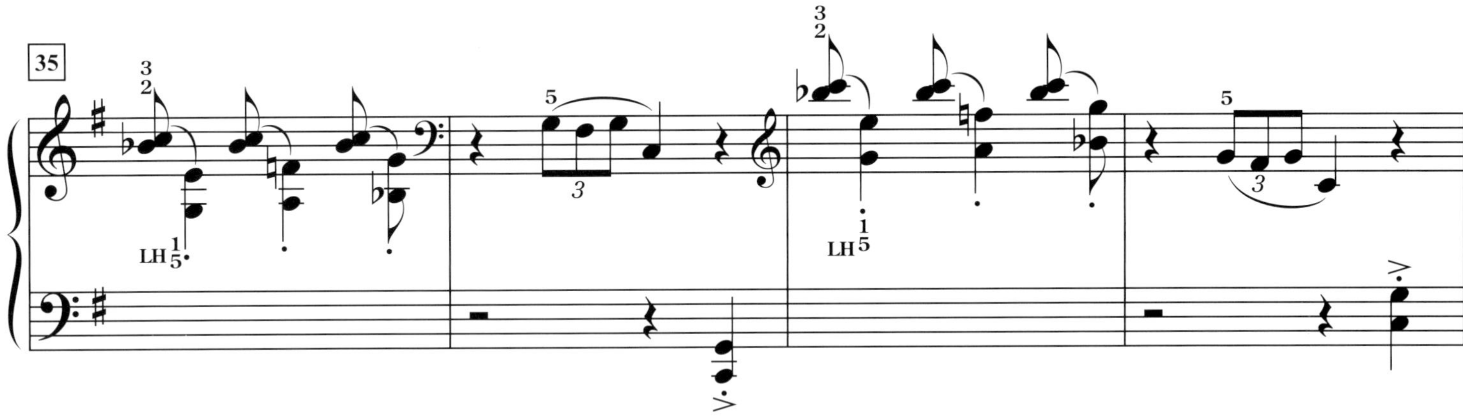

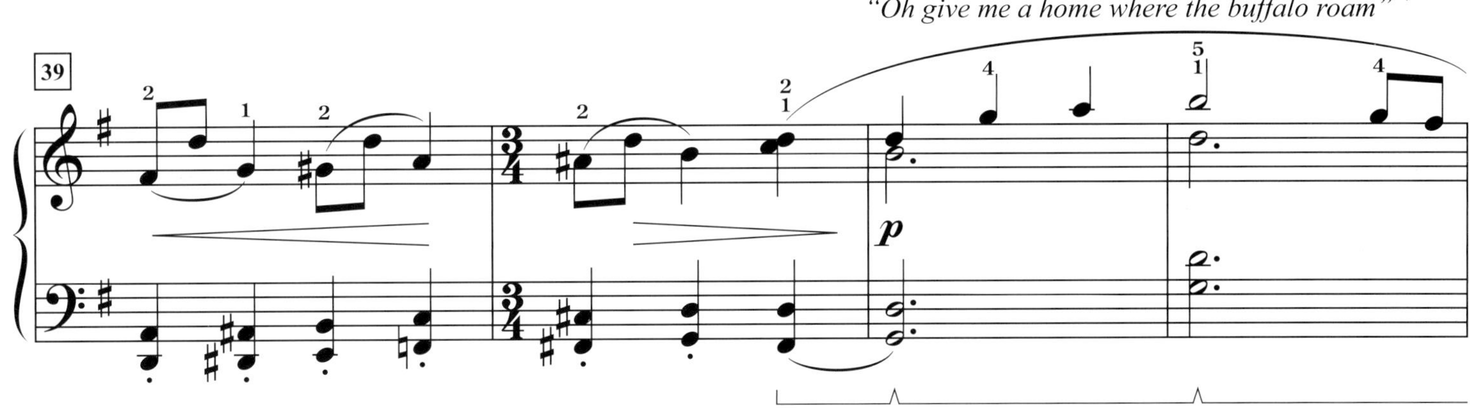

* Melody and lyrics from the popular American folk song "Home on the Range"

Jewel Cave

With 160 miles of mapped passages, Jewel Cave is the second-longest cave in the world. The wind is exceptionally strong in magnificent tunnels with nicknames like "Whistle Stop" and "Hurricane Corner." The jewels are the calcite crystals that cover the walls of this cave like diamonds! Notice the colorful harmonies and key changes that reflect this rich atmosphere.

Wynn-Anne Rossi

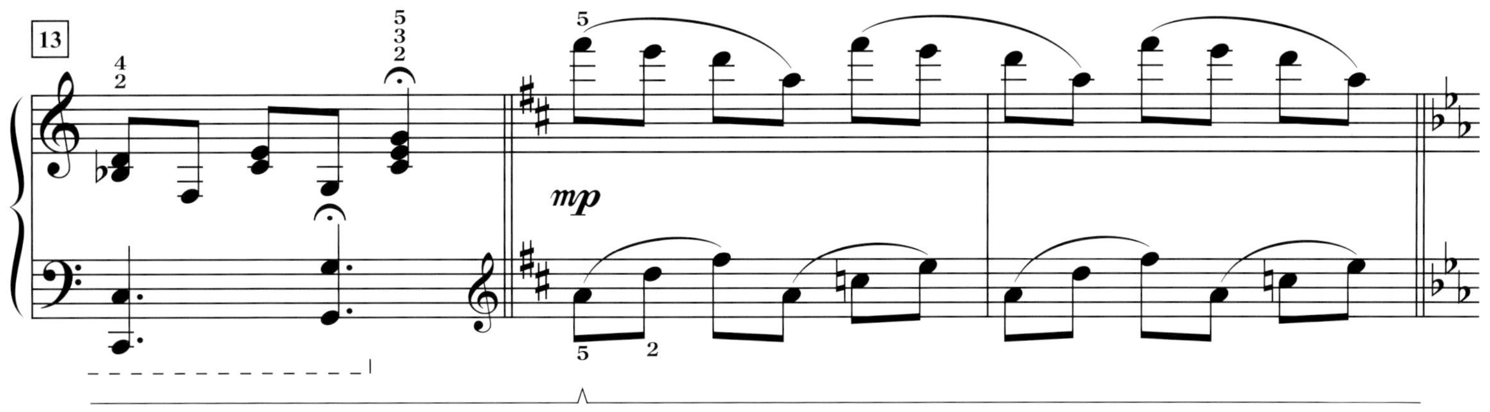
mp

f
8va

Majestic ceilings

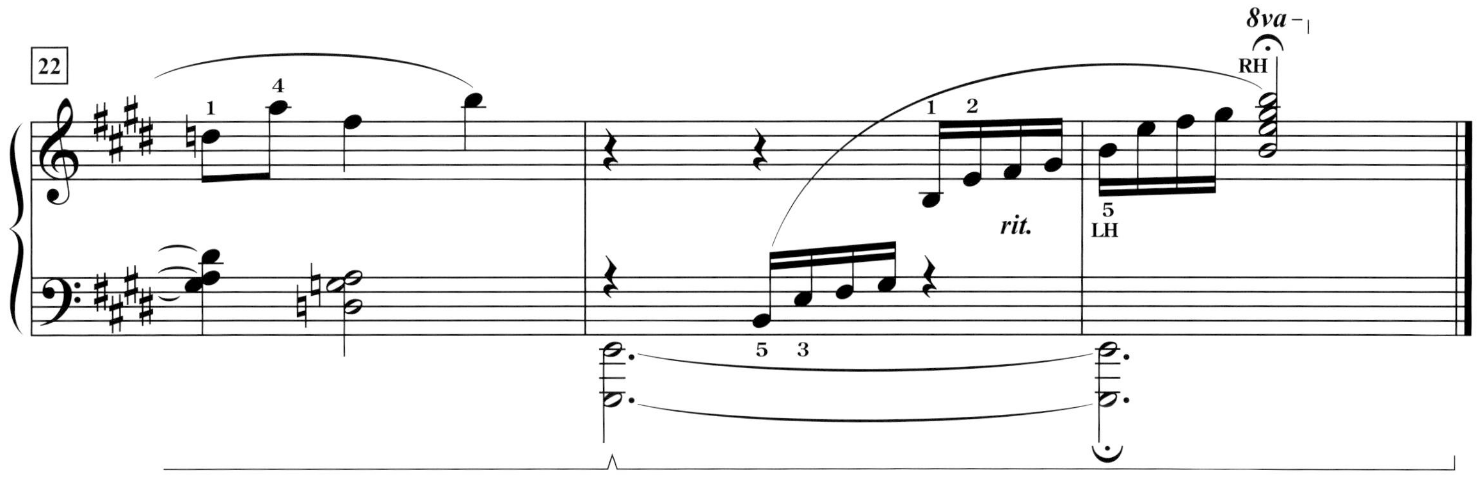
8va
RH
rit.
LH

Badlands Thunderstorm

The Badlands was difficult territory for the Lakota Indians, French trappers, and early explorers. Steep slopes, deep sand, sparse vegetation, and wild thunderstorms gave it the reputation of being a challenging land to cross. However, today's view is spectacular! Massive erosion has revealed millions of ancient fossils in a powerful landscape of magnificent color.

Wynn-Anne Rossi

22
27
32
37
42
mp
mf
f
cresc.
ff rit.

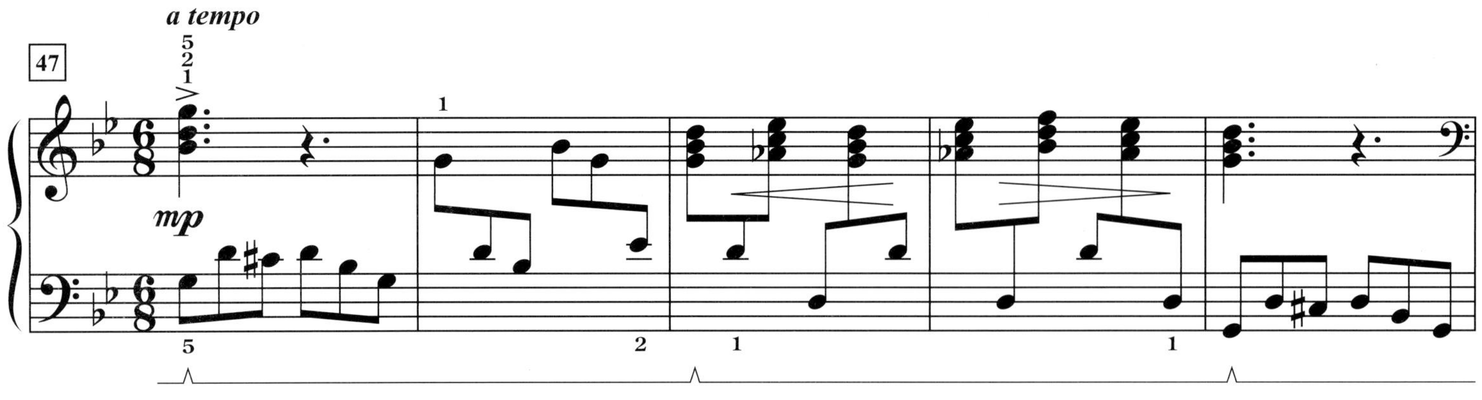

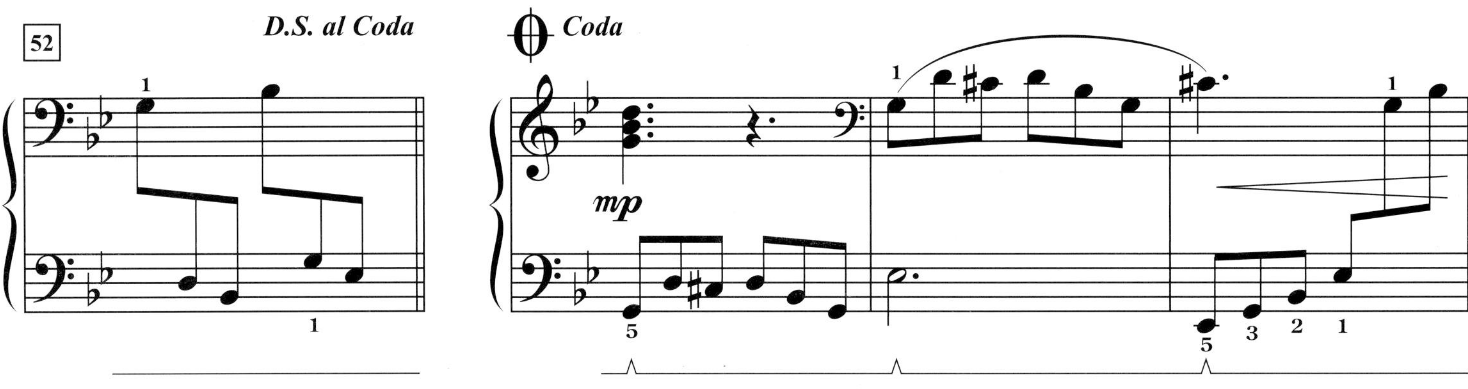

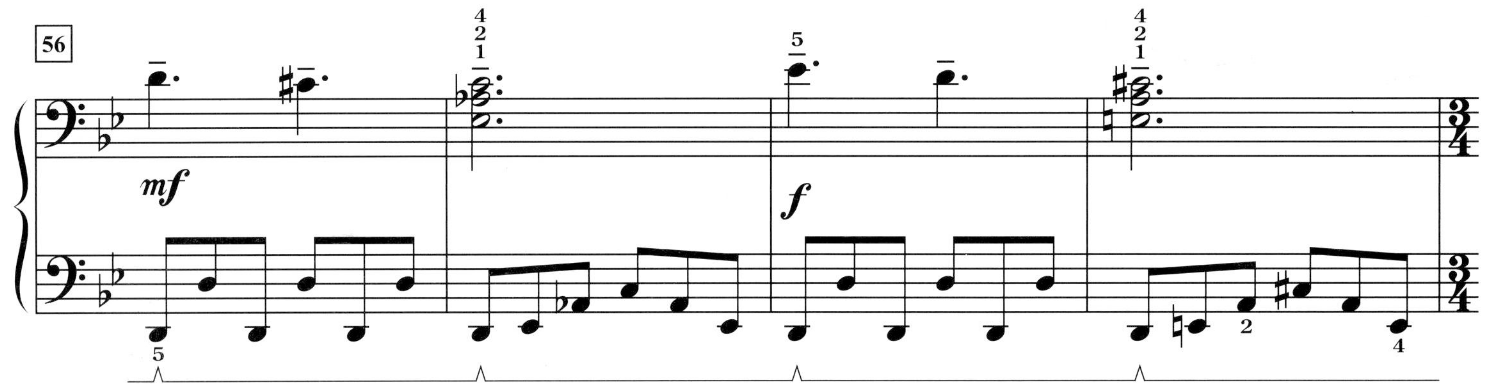

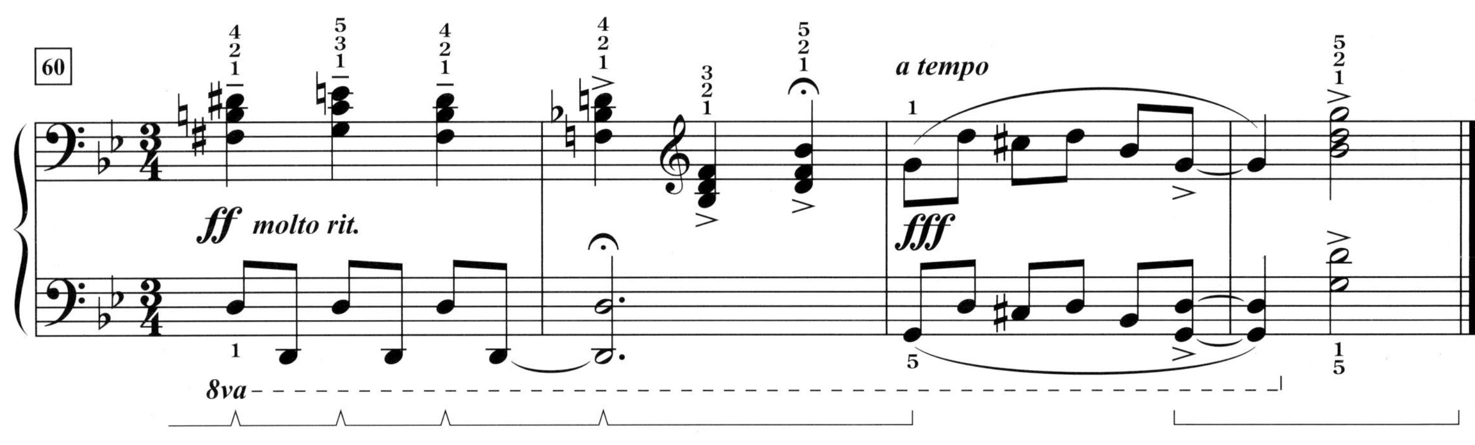

Cover Photos
Black Hills National Forest: © Shutterstock.com/Jason Patrick Ross • South Dakota Landscape: © Shutterstock.com/welcomia
Silhouette of a Bison: © Shutterstock.com/Tom Reichner

42445 US $4.50

alfred.com

ISBN-10: 1-4706-1114-7
ISBN-13: 978-1-4706-1114-9

PRINTED IN THE USA